AF444396

Top 100
MOST COMMON
INDONESIAN VERBS

Available on Amazon in paperback
And Kindle versions
And book stores
Copyright © Think Bahasa Pte Ltd 2020

WORD LIST | *Part 1*

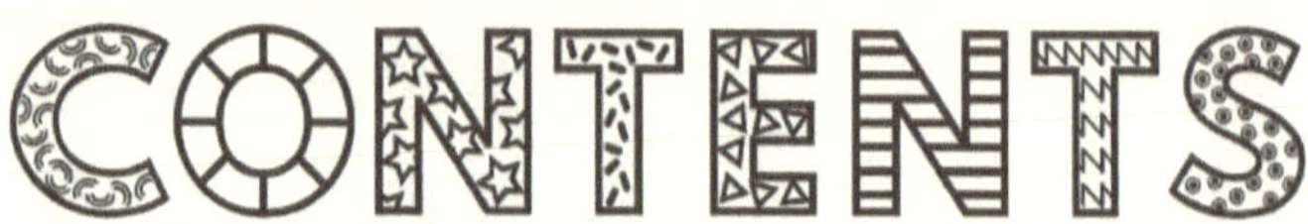

TO ADD

TO ANSWER

TO ASK

TO BATHE / TO SHOWER

TO BECOME

TO BEGIN / TO START

TO BELIEVE

TO BOIL

TO BORROW

TO BRING

TO BUILD

TO BUY

TO CALL

TO CHANGE

TO CLEAN

TO CLOSE

TO COME

TO CONTINUE

TO COOK

TO CRY

TO CUT

TO DECIDE

TO DO

TO DIVIDE

TO DRAW

WORD LIST | *Part 2*

CONTENTS

WORD LIST | *Part 3*

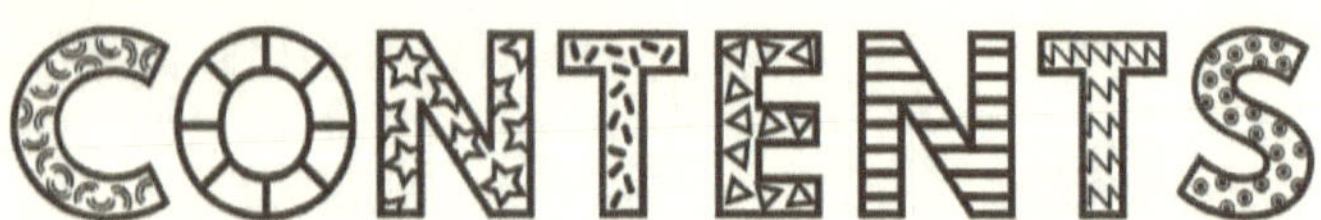

CONTENTS

TO NEED

TO OFFER

TO OPEN

TO PARK

TO PAY

TO PLAY

TO PREPARE

TO PULL

TO PUSH

TO PUT

TO READ

TO RECEIVE

TO REMEMBER

TO REST

TO RIDE

TO ROAST

TO RUN

TO SAY

TO SEE

TO SELL

TO SEND

TO SHAVE

TO SHOW

TO SING

TO SIT

WORD LIST | Part 4

CONTENTS

WHAT WE LEARN WITH PLEASURE, WE NEVER FORGET

Alfred Mercier

To add

TAMBAHKAN

Please **add** more sugar

Tolong **tambahkan** gula lebih banyak

To answer

JAWAB

I know how to **answer** her question

Saya tahu cara **jawab** pertanyaan dia

To ask

TANYA

You can **ask** me questions now

Kamu bisa **tanya** saya pertanyaan sekarang

To bathe / to shower

MANDI

I **shower** before I have breakfast

Saya **mandi** sebelum saya makan pagi

To become

MENJADI

I want **to become** a doctor

Saya mau **menjadi** seorang dokter

To begin / to start

MULAI

I **began** to read this book yesterday

Saya **mulai** baca buku ini kemarin

To believe

PERCAYA

I **believe** you

Saya **percaya** kamu

To boil

REBUS

Boil the water for 15 minutes

Rebus airnya selama 15 menit (lima belas)

To borrow

PINJAM

I need to **borrow** your pen

Saya perlu **pinjam** bolpoin kamu

To bring

BAWA

I will **bring** pizza to your party

Saya akan **bawa** pizza ke pesta kamu

To build

BANGUN

I want to **build** a new house

Saya mau **bangun** sebuah rumah baru

To buy

BELI

I **bought** my textbook yesterday

Saya **beli** buku cetak saya kemarin

To call

PANGGIL

You can **call** me Sarah

Kamu bisa **panggil** saya Sarah

To change

GANTI

I want to **change** to a bigger table

Saya mau **ganti** ke meja lebih besar

To clean

BERSIHKAN

I need to **clean** the table

Saya perlu **bersihkan** mejanya

To close

TUTUP

Can you **close** the door?

Bisakah kamu **tutup** pintunya?

To come

DATANG

I will **come** to the meeting later

Saya akan **datang** ke pertemuaannya nanti

To continue

LANJUTKAN

Let's **continue** watching TV

Mari **lanjutkan** nonton TV

To cook

MASAK

I can **cook** Indonesian food

Saya bisa **masak** makanan Indonesia

To cry

NANGIS

He **cries** like a baby

Dia **nangis** seperti bayi

To cut

POTONG

Cut this paper to 4 pieces

Potong kertas ini menjadi 4 bagian
(empat)

To decide

PUTUSKAN

I **decided** to go to Bali next month

Saya **putuskan** untuk pergi ke Bali
bulan depan

To do

LAKUKAN

What do you want **to do**?

Kamu mau **lakukan** apa?

To divide

BAGI

The teacher **divided** the students into four groups

Guru **bagi** para murid menjadi empat kelompok

To draw

GAMBAR

My daughter can **draw** a house

Anak perempuan saya bisa **gambar** rumah

To drink

MINUM

I do not **drink** soda

Saya tidak **minum** soda

To drive

SETIR

I **drive** to office every morning

Saya **setir** ke kantor setiap pagi

To dry

KERINGKAN

I like **to dry** my clothes outside

Saya suka **keringkan** baju saya di luar

To eat

MAKAN

I like **to eat** pasta

Saya suka <u>makan</u> pasta

To explain

JELASKAN

I need to **explain** to you

Saya perlu **jelaskan** ke kamu

To finish

SELESAI

I **finish** my work early

Saya **selesai** pekerjaan saya awal

To fly

TERBANG

Birds can **fly**

Burung bisa **terbang**.

To forget

LUPA

I **forgot** to bring my laptop

Saya **lupa** bawa laptop saya

To give

BERI / KASIH

Please **give** this money to Jose

Tolong **beri** uang ini ke Jose

To go

PERGI

I must **go** to Jakarta for work

Saya harus **pergi** ke Jakarta untuk pekerjaan

To hear

DENGAR

I cannot **hear** you

Saya tidak bisa **dengar** kamu

To help

BANTU

I can **help** you

Saya bisa **bantu** kamu

To hug

PELUK

I want to **hug** my friend

Saya mau **peluk** teman saya

To iron

SETRIKA

My daughter knows how to **iron** her clothes

Anak perempuan saya tahu cara **setrika** bajunya

To join

IKUT

Join me for breakfast tomorrow!

Ikut saya untuk makan pagi besok!

To jump

LOMPAT

I can **jump**

Saya bisa **lompat**

To keep

SIMPAN

You can **keep** my money first

Kamu bisa **simpan** uang saya dulu

To kiss

CIUM

My wife **kisses** my cheek every morning

Istri saya **cium** pipi saya setiap pagi

To know

TAHU

I **know** that she is lying

Saya **tahu** dia bohong

22

To leave

TINGGALKAN

Many guests have **left** the party

Banyak tamu sudah **tinggalkan** pestanya

To like

SUKA

I **like** chocolate

Saya **suka** coklat

To listen

DENGARKAN

I like to **listen** to FM8 radio

Saya suka **dengarkan** radio FM8

To make / to create

BUAT

I like to **make** scrapbook

Saya suka **buat** scrapbook

To meet

BERTEMU

I will **meet** her later

Saya akan **bertemu** dia nanti

To mix

CAMPURKAN

I don't like to **mix** sweet and sour food

Saya tidak suka **campurkan** makanan manis dan asam

To need

BUTUH / PERLU

I **need** to go

Saya **perlu** pergi

To offer

TAWARKAN

I **offer** the old lady to sit

Saya **tawarkan** perempuan tua itu duduk

To open

BUKA

<u>Open</u> your notes!

<u>Buka</u> catatan kamu!

To park

PARKIR

You cannot **<u>park</u>** here

Kamu tidak bisa **<u>parkir</u>** disini

To pay

BAYAR

You can **pay** this time

Kamu bisa **bayar** kali ini

To play

MAIN

Let's **play** outside

Mari **main** di luar

28

To prepare

SIAPKAN

My helper has already **prepared** dinner

Pembantu saya sudah **siapkan** makan malam

To pull

TARIK

Do not **pull** the rope

Jangan **tarik** talinya

To push

DORONG

Push the door

Dorong. pintunya

To put

TARUH

Please **put** my book on the table

Tolong **taruh** buku saya di atas meja

To read

BACA

I like to **read** book

Dorong. pintunya

To receive

TERIMA

I **received** your email last night

Saya **terima** email kamu tadi malam

To remember

INGAT

I **remember** his birthday

Saya **ingat** ulang tahunnya

To rest

ISTIRAHAT

I want to **rest** for a while

Saya mau **istirahat** sebentar

To ride

NAIK

I like to **ride** bike (bicycle)

Saya suka **naik** sepeda

To roast

PANGGANG

I like to **roast** a chicken

Saya suka **panggang**. ayam

To run

LARI

Run, now!

Lari, sekarang!

To say

BILANG

Don't **say** anything to her

Jangan **bilang** apapun ke dia

To see

LIHAT

I **<u>saw</u>** an accident on a highway

Saya **<u>lihat</u>** kecelakaan di jalan raya

To sell

JUAL

I **<u>sell</u>** my books online

Saya **<u>jual</u>** buku saya online

To send

KIRIM

I will **send** my application tomorrow

Saya akan **kirim** aplikasi saya besok

To shave

CUKUR

He needs to **shave** his beard

Dia perlu **cukur** janggutnya

36

To show

TUNJUKKAN

Please **show** me your passport!

Tolong **tunjukkan** saya paspor kamu

To sing

NYANYI

I like to **sing** Chinese songs

Saya suka **nyanyi** lagu Cina

To sit

DUDUK

I am **sitting** next to Michelle

Saya sedang **duduk** di sebelah Michelle

To sleep

TIDUR

I want to **sleep** early tonight

Saya mau **tidur** lebih awal malam ini

To smile

SENYUM

My baby likes to **smile**

Bayi saya suka **senyum**

To speak

BICARA

I **speak** Indonesian language fluently

Saya **bicara** Bahasa Indonesia dengan lancar

To stand

BERDIRI

I am **standing** near the door

Saya sedang **berdiri** di dekat pintu

To stir

ADUK

Stir the soup for 10 minutes

Aduk supnya selama 10 menit (sepuluh)

To stop

BERHENTI

Stop talking!

Berhenti bicara!

To study

BELAJAR

I **studied** Indonesian for 2 months

Saya **belajar** Bahasa Indonesia selama 2 bulan

To sweep

SAPU

I will **sweep** the floor later

Saya akan **sapu** lantainya nanti

To swim

RENANG

I can **swim**

Saya bisa **renang**.

To take

AMBIL

I **took** this pen from your room

Saya **ambil** pena ini dari kamar kamu

To think

PIKIR

I **think** the food is delicious

Saya **pikir** makanannya enak

To throw

LEMPAR

Throw the ball to him

Lempar bolanya ke dia

To try

COBA

I like to **try** new food

Saya suka **coba** makanan baru

To turn off

MATIKAN

Turn of the radio!

Matikan radionya!

To turn on

NYALAKAN

Turn on the light!

Nyalakan lampunya!

To type

KETIK

I can **type** very fast without looking

Saya bisa **ketik** sangat cepat tanpa melihat

To use

PAKAI

I **use** spoon and fork to eat

Saya **pakai** sendok dan garpu untuk makan

46

To wait

TUNGGU

I can **wait**

Saya bisa **tunggu**

To wake up

BANGUN

I **wake** up early today

Saya **bangun** awal hari ini

To walk

JALAN

I like to <u>walk</u> to my office

Saya suka <u>jalan</u> ke kantor saya

To want

INGIN

I **want** to eat

Saya **mau** makan

To wash

CUCI

I **wash** my clothes later

Saya **cuci** pakaian saya nanti

To watch

NONTON

I like to **watch** movie

Saya suka **nonton** film

To work

KERJA

I **work** three hours a day

Saya **kerja** tiga jam sehari

To write

TULIS

I **wrote** this letter for my mother

Saya **tulis** surat ini untuk Ibu saya

Find a large
collection of
bilingual <u>English
Indonesian books</u>
at a variety of
reading levels
only at:

WWW.INDONESIANSTORYBOOKS.COM

INDONESIAN TONGUE TWISTER

Improve your pronunciation in Indonesian. This book is a fantastic resource to use as an articulation practice for Indonesian as Second Language Learners!

INDONESIAN INTERNET SLANG WORDS & ACRONYMS

Learn colloquial Indonesian. This book is perfect to learn and teach uses of Indonesian in informal setting, particularly the use of acronyms and abbreviations when texting and communicating via mobile phone and social media.